Interviewing Quick Guide:
The Art and Craft

by Drew Becker

Drew Becker

Book 1 Interviewing Quick Guide: The Art and Craft

Book 2 Write a Non-Fiction Book in 4 Weeks

All Rights Reserved. No part of this publication may be reproduced in any form or by any means, including scanning, photocopying, or otherwise without prior written permission of the copyright holder.
Copyright Drew Becker © 2016

SBN-10:1-944662-10-3

ISBN-13:978-1-944662-10-3

Cover Art by Rockbrand Creative Jennifer Davis

Dedication

Interviewing Quick Guide is dedicated to my writing mentors, influential teachers and fellow writers along the way. Thanks to Elementary School Teachers Mr. Maine and Mr. Chapman; Mr. Rothstein, Ms. Hunt and Mr. Daly at George Washington High School; Mr. John Visvader and Mr. John Wrenn at the University of Colorado; Brian and Leslie Brown in Aiken, South Carolina, and numerous North Carolina writers with whom I have collaborated over the years.

I don't know exactly what inspired me to ask questions but I have always had the inclination to ask. I owe this to many teachers, parents and siblings who have challenged me over the years to learn more. Interviews and less formal questioning have allowed me to go where I could not go myself and added to the breadth of my knowledge.

And never-ending praise for my wife who puts up with all my moods as I take on writing projects. Her patience is truly amazing.

Table of Contents

A Little About the Series and Me 1

What's It All About? 5

What Do You Want and How Can You Get It? 9

How Do You Do It? 19

How Do You Know That? 33

Why vs. Did You Know 39

What, When, Who? & Beyond 45

Say What? 55

The Answers 63

Can we Get a Checklist? 71

Last Words 77

Acknowledgments

Thanks to the numerous interviewers I have watched including late night TV hosts, investigative journalists, Charlie Rose, Barbara Walters, Dick Cavett, Larry King and others on television. Thanks also to Misty Campbell who has worked with me over the years doing video interviews and who was a TV news producer. I call her the "Queen of Questions" because she is always ready with another question in interviews when I think they all have been asked. I appreciate the time Pam Orren took to talk with me about techniques she uses in her social work.

I wish to also mention others who have been helpful. Lawrence Harte gave me the opportunity to run the video committee for the Digital Marketing for Business conference in 2014. Conducting numerous interviews with speakers was invaluable in my learning. Claudio Niedworok interviewed me about e-publishing and poetics on Claudio's SpeakEasy & Radio Theatre. Pat Howlett has interviewed me a couple of times on his Blogtalk radio show as well. Each of these experiences added to my personal knowledge of interviewing.

I wish to thank my lovely wife, Diana Henderson, who has seen much less of me while I completed this book. She is also my editor and has a keen eye and strong skills to see what I have overlooked.

Introduction

Most of us have watched interviews on *60 Minutes*, on late night TV, on ESPN or on entertainment shows where reporters or interviewers talk with celebrities. The process is usually fluid and seems to be spontaneous, but if you have ever tried to interview someone off the cuff, you have probably learned that it is not so simple. Jimmy Fallon and other talk show hosts usually have a deck of index cards where the questions are written. These help to create that flow we take for granted.

What if you want to be a good interviewer? Can you go to school to do that? Well, you might study it in a journalism class or may learn interrogation techniques if you are in the certain positions in the armed service or a detective, but there are no specific courses I have found that teach you how to do this. A few articles on the web might be somewhat helpful but I know of no great resources.

Since I wanted to know, I decided to research and write this book. In addition to scouring the web for information, I spoke with a former news producer who conducted interviews in the field and a social worker who uses interviews as a way to gather client information. I also examined my own interviewing techniques from my experiences as the interviewer and as the person being interviewed.

Many of you will be doing interviews using webcams and Google Hangouts or Skype, and I hope this book is helpful for you as well.

Chapter 1
A Little About the Series and Me

In this series, I intend to share my knowledge and experiences. This first book, *Interviewing Quick Guide: The Art and Craft,* is intended to help writers and other interviewers and their subjects have the best interviewing experience as possible. I hope you enjoy the book and the process.

You might wonder why I would write a book like this. It dawned on me some time ago that there is an art to conducting an interview.

I have been a writer for over 40 years and have my own marketing company, Convey Media Group. We help clients, especially independent authors and innovators, with social media and video as well as branding and other traditional marketing. In retrospect, I realize I have been interviewing folks for most of those years whether gathering software requirements as a technical writing in a major corporation or while working as a video producer for promotional videos.

Drew Becker

I ran the video committee for the Digital Marketing For Business conference and our group did video interviews with most of the speakers. As I worked with my committee members, some were more comfortable handling these interviews than others. Some interviewers felt more in their element because they had an understanding of the technology. Others seemed to draw comfort from their ability to prepare questions that would set the interviewee at ease.

I realized that there were a few tips and techniques that helped many of the interviewers.

This book is my attempt to share some of that knowledge with you so you can up your game the next time you do an interview. Although we did not find any hard and fast rules, the experience did provide some important clues to increase the interviewer's comfort and run smoother sessions.

* * *

I have always been a writer. Before college I worked in the shipping department of a clothing distributor and was scribbling on the *Inspected by* scraps. After college, when driving a taxicab, I would take a few minutes between fares to write in my notebook.

In the corporate world, I worked as a technical writer, marketing writer, a software support specialist and in sales, and I always found a way to record something during the day—even if only at my lunch break. Writing is in my blood because I have ideas floating around my head almost every day and think some of them might be valuable to others.

I know that you have these flitting ideas as well, and I hope that you are or will begin to capture them. You might only record a phrase or word, but jot down enough to examine your thoughts later and decide whether they're worthy of working up into something more.

My vision for the world is that we live in a less stressful, less conflicted environment. I believe that when someone is busy creating, he or she has little time to criticize others or increase that discord. If writers are not happy with the world around them, they create their own. The world can be a better place if people find and practice their unique creative talents.

I left the corporate world just after the events of 9/11 shifted the business climate. I was caught in the wake of circumstances that shortly followed: The company where I worked had been recently acquired by another and that corporation used the event as a rationale to cut most of us working at their satellite location. I was devastated but decided the time had come to strike out on my own. I'd lived in the shadows of one corporate giant or government organization for most of my working life. This time I decided that if anyone would fire me, it would be me.

I also teach writing classes and mentor writing clients. The *Writers Block Book Series* is based on many of the lessons I have learned from those experiences and participants. As a former English teacher, before emigrating to the world of business, I had a good foundation in grammar and spelling as well as in composition and logic. I continue to take courses and learn about the art of writing, the craft of publishing both electronic (e-books) and traditional books, marketing and sales, and social psychology.

Chapter 2

What's It All About?

The Essentials

So, you want to conduct an interview, either for a promotional video or to write an article or to share with your audience the knowledge of a well-known or obscure person. You have all watched numerous interviews on TV and listened to them on the radio. You have listened to interviews on your computer on BlogTalk radio. Most of you have had a job interview during which you have had to answer questions from prospective employers. The thing is though, that as a rule, you never were taught how to conduct an interview. Although there is a plethora of books about how to answer questions, the material about how to conduct an interview is sparse. Public schools do not offer classes in the subject. You learn to stand up and give speeches in speech class but the only place you might learn interviewing skills is in a journalism class or working on the school newspaper.

So I looked around for a source for preparing an interview rather than for how to prepare to be interviewed and could find only a few books, none of which was succinct and helpful. I realized I could help people who are interested in interviewing by creating a concise, quick-to-read book.

This book is for anyone who wants to improve interviewing skills and get the most from your guests. I refer to the people being interviewed as guests because I believe anyone I interview deserves to be treated like a guest in my own home. The book also has tips for making interviewing easy by following a number of suggestions. With these ideas and attitudes, you should never be caught off-guard by the person you interview and when the interview is complete, your guest should feel grateful. When you generate this kind of good will, your guest in many cases may help you to secure your next interview if you ask.

Why I wrote Interviewing Quick Guide

I recently led the Video committee for a conference called Digital Marketing for Business. Members of my committee interviewed the upcoming speakers using Google Hangouts. We found that one of the major differences between successful and not-as-successful interviews was preparation. Some volunteers seemed naturally to be more ready when interviewing. I had provided a set of standard questions for each interviewer but the results were uneven. I reviewed the interviews after the conference and realized some people were more comfortable than others. I wondered what was the difference in these interviews.

Preparation was the answer. Even though being comfortable with the questions was key, other skills related to preparation were also important. Beyond being prepared the better interviewers also had knowledge about what to prepare and how to use preparations to get better interviews and videos.

What Will You Need?

You will learn about the tools and technology you need in order to conduct a video or audio interview as well as a face-to-face interview that you will later use to write a blog, article or part of a book. The technology in each of these is different, so I will let you know what you need in each case. I have done interviews with nothing more than a pencil or pen and a notebook, and I have done interviews where the webcam for the guest and myself needed to be set up and tested beforehand. When conducting a live video interview, we would bring a wagon-full of equipment.

The type of interview determines the tools and technology and your tools, in part, determine some of your preparation for that particular interview. Look at the *How Do You Do That* chapter for more information about your tools and technology.

How to Prepare

Have I mentioned how important it is to prepare? The better prepared you are for the interview, the more you can focus on your guest and stop worrying about what you will ask next. You will want to look at the chapters on preparation to learn how to be ready for your interview. These chapters include tips on what kinds of questions to ask, how to ask those questions, what to do with the answers and other important components of preparation.

A Tool to Use (Checklist)

I have also included a tool that may be helpful in conducting your interviews. You can find this checklist at the end of the book useful. I hope readers will send feedback and add other ideas on the website *http://drewbecker.com/?p=1132* where you will be able to see updates to the book and additional information as you, the readers, share your experiences.

Read on to begin your journey and learn about different facets of the interview.

Chapter 3

What Do You Want and How Can You Get It?

When you decide to do your interview, you might want to answer two questions yourself. First, what is the purpose of the interview, and, second, what can you do to get the most poignant, revealing and fascinating answers. To get the best out of the interview, you need to do preliminary thinking even before you begin your planning.

Purpose

The first consideration when thinking about an interview is what you want to share with your readers or viewers. This is the purpose of the interview. Do you want to use the interview to promote a person or event? Do you want to entertain or is your focus more about providing information? How personal do you want the interview to be, and how open is your guest to revealing him or herself? Where will the interview be seen or read?

To answer these questions, we need to begin with the audience. Are you writing or producing for a family-friendly publication or outlet? Will this be seen on YouTube where you do not know who your audience is? Is your interview for a specific industry or niche? Will it be available to the general public, to pre-selected groups or only to paid or unpaid subscribers? If you do not know who your primary and secondary audiences are, it is much more difficult to prepare and conduct a great interview.

If your audience is stay-at-home moms and dads, your questions will be different from those you would prepare if your interview is for a business-to-business publication or network. In the first case, you will direct your guest towards topics that interest them centered on home and family and children's activities. You would not ask how a government regulation is affecting the safety standards in small manufacturing plants; that topic would be more beneficial in an industry-specific venue. On the other hand, in a promotional interview, you would rarely ask about the best ways to get children to brush their teeth (unless, of course, your work is for a family dental practice).

I know all this seems obvious, but numerous interviews have gone awry because the interviewer strayed from the purpose.

Language

Another important consideration is the language you use. Take into account your audience. Is your interview going to be read, heard or seen by children, young adults, families, or by adults only? Depending on which of these audiences you address, you will need to pay attention to how you phrase certain things. The background of the guest is also important.

Will people who listen, watch or read your interview be native English speakers, or will you have an international audience? Certain phrases and words may be confusing to those for whom English is not their primary language.

The depth of knowledge your audience has should determine how much jargon and which industry-specific terms you use. If in doubt, be sure to ask your guest to define terms. You can establish the kinds of answers to a certain extent by the questions you prepare and your follow-up comments and questions.

Setting up the Right Environment

You can do the best preparation in the world for your interview but if your guest is not comfortable, your interview will flop. So what does it take to relax your guest so that he or she will give you a great interview? Prepare him or her in your meeting prior to the interview, just before the interview and during the interview.

Prior

When possible have a meeting a week or more before your scheduled interview. In this meeting set the limits for the interview, decide on length, discuss topics, take some notes about points to be covered and explain what the process will be like. This casual meeting also will help your guest get more comfortable with you as you spend time together. This meeting should be your opportunity to deepen or establish good rapport with your guest. Take advantage of this chance to set a friendly tone that can spill over into the interview itself. You also will want to ask for a profile/biography from your guest that you can use as an introduction. The profile content may help when you do research as well. Be aware that some interviewees will want to write or send a prepared bio while others may prefer to talk it through and have you write it. If your guest chooses the latter approach, be sure to give the person a chance to see your written bio before using it.

Some guests will not answer certain questions; knowing these beforehand is helpful especially for a live or video interview. You can avoid uncomfortable pauses—especially on video—if you steer clear of these questions. Creating trust with people you interview is key to getting them to open up and share those brilliant insights that can change an average interview into a phenomenal one. The exception to this tip is if your interview is investigative in nature, which means you need to ask confrontational questions. In that case you probably will not meet prior to the interview. In other cases, however, defining the mine fields can prevent sabotaging the event. Of course, this does not mean you cannot ask unexpected questions.

Share four or five of the questions you will ask. These can be general questions like "What is your inspiration?" or "How did you accomplish this or that?" These questions can help relax the guest during the interview. Guests become uncomfortable when they are not in control. If they generally know what to expect in the way of questions, the experience will be easier for them.

You may want to have the guest sign release forms during this preliminary meeting. If you are filming video at their place of business, home, etc., a location agreement protects you by having written proof that you had permission to use that venue. It is more difficult to get these signed after you have completed the interview.

Discuss logistics. Let them know when you are coming, what equipment you are bringing, how much time is required for setup, what electrical needs you have and how many people are coming with you on the day of the interview. This is less critical when you are doing a face-to-face interview that will be written up later than it is when you are doing a video interview at their location. If they are coming to you, be sure they have good directions, know what time to be there, and make certain that you have exchanged contact information in case something comes up or they need help to find your location.

For a video interview, talk about what they should wear. Will you be shooting from the waist up or will you also be shooting additional footage (B-roll) where you film them walking around the facility or in front of a group? Bring up make-up. Let them know if you are shooting on their location that furniture or other things may need to be moved. Assure them you will reconstruct their room when you are finished.

When shooting video, we usually use at least a two-person team. One person will shoot and the other will produce and direct. Sometimes it may be just one person. In other cases you may use a whole crew. Prepare your guest. We tell them beforehand to wear solid colors, pastel to dark. The best color for many people is navy blue, but if your guest knows what colors look best on him or her, let them wear those as long as they are solid. Avoid black and white when possible. If shooting full shots, their pants should be solid colors again like navy, tan or black. As far as makeup advice, tell women to put their makeup on a little darker than usual for the camera. Let both men and women know that you may apply powder if their faces or foreheads are shiny on camera.

Just Before

To help the guest feel comfortable, you must be at ease. Make sure you have allotted extra time to set everything up and get the crew or yourself settled. Center yourself before you begin working with the guest so they can see you are relaxed and know what you are doing. Being professional will help create the right atmosphere.

During the interview

Again, in order for your guest to be comfortable, you have to be. Stay tuned in to your guest. Ignore any distractions and maintain eye contact so your guest feels like he or she is talking only with you.

Be sure to smile; it puts both of you at ease.

Phone interviews and podcasts via the internet are inherently more challenging since you cannot see your guest's visual cues. This means you need to listen intently both to tone and what is being said. It requires a higher level of focus since you need to keep track of verbal cues and subtle changes in tone by listening between the lines.

A Challenging Shoot

One of the most challenging video shoots that my partner and I did was with a certain client. Let's call him John. He is a great guy and fun to be around. We were in a networking group together. John was a natural introvert, and when he stood in front of people he would stammer when he spoke. One-on-one, he was a little better, but he had difficulty expressing himself. Sometimes he would stutter and people had to be patient to hear what he would say. When we approached him about a video, he was reluctant and reminded us of his difficulties communicating. We assured him we could get good footage of him and produce a great promotional video.

He took a long time to agree but finally decided to do his videos. We had our preliminary meeting with him and jotted down lots of notes, but more importantly, we saw him in his natural surroundings and we all got to know each other better. By the end of the meeting, he was sharing his hobbies and we were smiling and telling jokes. The three of us became friends in a few hours.

The day of the video shoot we showed up at his home office and set up. We chatted as we set up the lights and camera and rearranged the room for optimal video. He was nervous but we could feel the trust from him. We assured him we had plenty of time, batteries and film to shoot and that he could have as many takes as necessary to in order to get the video we needed. We helped him pick the shirts that would look best for the different shots, and I talked him through the questions as my video partner Misty put on his powder.

He was perspiring quite a bit so throughout the interview we stopped and reapplied powder as needed. Before each shot, Misty would adjust his shirt so that we could see no wrinkles. He liked the attention and his trust increased as we continued through the session. Each time we filmed, his presentation got better and better with fewer pauses and less stammering. I don't remember how many takes we did, but in the end, we had enough footage. John presented himself professionally and did a great job of letting people know how conscientious and dedicated he was to his clients.

By the time we filmed the B-roll, video of him doing his work at this desk, talking with clients and showing us his garden, he was having a great time, and although I'm sure he was glad to have the filming done, he did tell us how much he enjoyed the afternoon.

Trust was what allowed us to get John on camera with minimal speech challenges. We began to establish this at our preliminary meeting and built it during the interim between that meeting and the filming. During the shoot his trust allowed him to relax and give us his best. With masterful cutting and post production, his promotional video came out fine and he was pleased with it. We worked hard on that project, but we learned along with John that even a naturally introverted and speech-challenged individual could be interviewed in such a way as to minimize weaknesses and produce a great result.

Drew Becker

Notes

Chapter 4
How Do You Do It?

No matter what kind of interview you are conducting, you will need some tools and in many cases technology. In this chapter I will discuss tools and technology for three types of interviews:

- The live interview used for writing a story, article or blog
- The sound interview for podcasting, BlogTalkRadio, or other sound production
- The phone interview
- The live sessions with video cameras
- The video interview using webcams
- The E-mail interview

Each of these situations needs a different set of tools and deserves to be discussed on its own. I will begin with the live interview to use for a written interview.

In 1967, Albert Mehrabian stated that in messages that are about feelings and attitudes, 7% of the meaning is conveyed with words, 38% in tone and 55% through visual cues. Although these numbers since have been questioned since, and the specific percentages may not hold up under scientific investigation, we can learn some important facts about communication. The words themselves (i.e., the written material of the interview) convey a small percentage of the message. Thus, a good writer/interviewer must be concise and interpretive when writing up an interview. When listening to a podcast or other sound interview, the listener is probably getting about half or a little more of the full communication. Even with a video interview, many of the nuances you could see in person are lost. All these factors lead me to the conclusion that the best interviewers must be extremely clear in what they produce.[1]

Upon completion of the interview, whenever possible, I offer to send a preliminary copy of the article or provide a preview of the broadcast to my guest before publication. I do this to be sure I have represented him or her accurately and as a courtesy.

The Live Interview (No Cameras)

Let's begin with the live interview. I recently talked with a renowned fashion photographer, Gordon Munro, for a local magazine. He had created a gallery in the front of his studio where he showed his work and that of other artists as well. We talked for over two hours, and he thanked me for an enjoyable afternoon at the end. I brought pen and paper and a digital recorder.

A live interview used to produce a written story at a later time requires the fewest tools and technology. I brought pen and paper and a digital recorder. Gordon and I talked for over two hours, and at the end he thanked me for an enjoyable afternoon.

To prepare for a live interview, be sure you have the tools you need. I dressed comfortably so I could sit anywhere to work.

Tools you might bring include:

1. Pens and pencils

2. A legal tablet with plenty of paper

3. Padfolio on which to write

4. A digital recorder (optional)

5. Laptop or digital tablet (optional)

Please bring more than one pencil or pen with you during an interview. Backup writing utensils are critical. You never want to have to stop an interview because the pen ran out of ink or the pencil lead broke. If you have to ask your guest for a writing utensil, he or she well may have doubts about your professionalism. Unfortunately, early in my career, I learned this the hard way, and when I asked the person I was interviewing for a pencil, saw a fleeting look of surprise on her face, and the interview went downhill from there. I was unable to write up the interview afterwards because my lack of preparation undermined my credibility and her replies became short and curt.

Have you ever had a meeting and were taking notes only to find you ran out of paper? One solution, of course, is to write on the back of pages you have already filled but this method is cumbersome and may distract your guest. Be sure to have plenty of paper. I carry an extra pad to all interviews.

When I went in to interview Gordon, we sat in a couple of overstuffed chairs in his gallery. Fortunately I had a padfolio to use as a writing surface. As you probably know, this is a leather or leather-like folder that holds a pad of paper, some pockets to keep other items, a spot for a pen and possibly other pockets suitable for carrying passports, magazines and other papers. You can purchase a padfolio for $15-20 USD at the low end and may pay over $100 USD for a high-end leather version. I suggest you get a letter or A4 size rather than the smaller 5" x 8" version. Flipping pages often can create a major distraction.

I take a digital recorder to my interviews so I can take sparse notes and focus on my guest. Afterwards I go back and replay the interview to write the article. Sometimes an inflection of voice reveals something the notes I took did not convey and adds additional insight into a comment. This can enhance an interview in ways you never expected. This nuance then can be explained in the written piece.

Another important reason to record is to validate what I thought I heard and to listen more than once to answers to be sure I am getting the information correctly. When I interviewed the poet, Allen Ginsberg, about Neil Cassidy in the 1970's, I recorded the interview. When it was published in The Denver Post, he read it and sent me a postcard. It was a City Lights postcard from the bookstore that published his poetry books. On the back he thanked me for accurately reporting what he had said during the session. He added that he had been misquoted so many times that he had been reluctant to do interviews. Recording the interview helped me stay true to my guest and write an accurate and informative article. I took great care writing that interview and must have been mindful of Albert Mehrabian's 7% word communication statement.

If you decide to go high tech and use a laptop or a digital tablet, be ready for possible snafus. Make sure the device is fully charged and will last through the interview. Bring a charging cable or cord in case you have to plug it in. I also bring an analogue backup (paper and pen).

The Sound Interview

An interview for a podcast, for BlogTalkRadio or for a sound file to be placed on a website requires some equipment to capture the session. To create any of these forms, it is important that you capture the sound with as much quality as possible.

Let me talk a little technical with you for a moment about bitrate. This is important to know. This nuance then can be explained in the written piece., it usually will be translated to an MP3 when loaded onto your source. You may record as an MP3 or as a Wave file but in either case, your final recording will be compressed to make the file size manageable. A standard CD holds about 70 minutes of music as a high-quality product. A CD can accomodate about 640 MB (megabytes) of information. When that sound is compressed into MP3 format, the size is greatly reduced, and, depending on how much compression there is, the quality is also reduced. Since most of your interviews will not include music, these higher quality levels are not necessary in the final product. The compression can be judged by bitrate.

Bitrate is the number of bits (binary digits) that are transferred over a certain period of time. Bitrates for sound are usually measured as a number of kilobytes per second (KBps). To obtain the best audio, record at the highest bitrate you can.

You can then compress the file to a lower bitrate to reduce the size. The highest bitrate is 320KBps, which is useful for music and voice. Record at this rate or 225KBps to get the best quality recording. Afterwards you will compress it to a lower bitrate

Here's a comparison of bitrates and file sizes:

- For 96KBps each minute will take 701 Kilobytes(KB)
- For 64 KBps each minute will take 456 KB
- For 32 KBbs each minute will take 230 KB

For speech and low-quality streaming, 96KBps is fine. 64KBbs is useful for speech but less clear, and 32KBbs is acceptable for speech. You will have to create compressed files, and listen to figure out what bitrate you are going to need.

What is important when you go into your interview to record is that you are getting the highest possible quality so that you can compress it later.

Enough techie stuff; let's get back to equipment.

Tools you might need are:

- A high-quality microphone
- A higher end digital recorder
- A higher quality webcam (if you are going to extract sound from video)

One of your first considerations will be a good microphone that will work on your computer. Spend a little more and get better sound quality than with a headset. Most headsets do not produce high-quality sound. I use an Audio Technica ATR2100 USB microphone which connects to a USB connector on my computer. I use this with my webcam interviews as well. If you are going to create a sound file from a webcast, test your source and the source of your guest first to be sure your digital files are high quality.

Invest in a good digital recorder if you are going to conduct interviews in person. When I began recording interviews ten years ago, I used a micro digital recorder. I found this useful when writing an article, but the quality was not good enough to publish. A few years ago, I purchased a larger but portable digital recorder (ZoomH4). It can record in MP3 or Wave format. I use the MP3 setting and adjust it to 128KBs for my recordings. I connect to a mini-stand and can plug into any AC outlet or run from batteries. Whenever I decide I will not be able to plug into an outlet, I bring 3-4 extra pairs of batteries. It is a distraction to have to reload batteries, but stopping a session to go out and buy more will usually destroy the interview for all but the friendliest guest.

The Phone Interview

The phone interview is inherently more challenging since you cannot see your guest's visual cues. For phone interviews, be sure your recorder has a standard microphone input plug (or adapter).

Along with the tools for a sound interview, you will need a telephone pickup for your voice recorder which connects into the phone and into your recorder. This is an older technology which means the recordings are usually a low sound quality and not nearly good enough to create a podcast. If I were to record phone conversations I might need an adapter to connect a standard to a 3.5mm mini plug.

Many phone interviews are now done with computers using services like BlogTalkRadio. You could also extract the audio from a webcam session. I will discuss webcams in the next section.

The Face-to-Face Video Interview

There are two types of video interviews, the computer-based and live in person. Each has its advantages and challenges.

The most personal way to do a video interview is in person, face to face. I usually work with one other person, and one of us will direct/produce while the other takes on the videographer tasks. Preparing lighting, audio and setting up the correct angles to film is crucial.

At a minimum you will need:

- your video camera

- a tripod
- lighting equipment- lights and stands or on-board lights
- microphones- lavalier, camera mounted and perhaps others
- extra batteries and media for recording

I find that using a prosumer camera is helpful. When we shoot, we use a Sony HXR-NX-30U which has built-in steady shot to reduce camera motion, great light sensitivity, manual and automatic adjustments, XLR audio inputs and other professional features. You can use a consumer camera but may not get as high-quality results.

No matter which camera, lights and sound equipment you choose, become familiar with all of these before you conduct your interview. Arrive early and plan on spending one-half to three-quarters of an hour to do professional setup. Bring backup equipment as well if you have it. Be sure the camera is charged and you have extra batteries, extension cords (stringers) and electrical strips for lights, backup batteries for any remote microphones, a toolkit with gaffer and other types of tape, scissors, and anything else you may need for setup.

The Video Interview Webcam

Computer-based interviews allow you to work with people outside your locale while live video interviews allow you to share your guest's surroundings with the audience or set up an optimal environment.

Let's look at the computer-based interview first. These are most often done with webcams. You will want as high a quality webcam as you can afford, and if this is a significant part of your business you will probably invest in a few more that you can mail to your guests to use for the interviews to be sure that the quality of the picture and sound is adequate.

The two products you can use that use without paying are Skype and Google Hangouts. With either of these services, you will need to have installations on your computer and that of your guest's. Anyone with a Google account has the option of using Hangouts. For Skype, both parties must go to their website and download the software (http://skype.com/en). Both you and the guest will need a webcam and/or headphones and a camera attached to the computer.

You will want to test the equipment before you do the interview especially if you expect an audience. Do a test run with your guest and check for lighting, sound and background. I will not cover using Google Hangouts or Skype in this book but there are many resources on the web to learn these technologies.

The E-Mail Interview

One last method of doing an interview is via e-mail. You can use this method with guests anywhere in the world, and you do not have to arrange a time or place. To conduct this type of interview, prepare a set of questions and e-mail to the guest. Use his or her answers to write the interview. I think offering to send a preliminary copy of the article before publication is most important for this type of interview because you have no face-to-face time, nor did your guest get to participate in the creation of the article as directly.

[1] http://www.businessballs.com/mehrabiancommunications.htm

Notes

Drew Becker

Notes

Chapter 5
How Do You Know That?

Once you have scheduled your interview and assembled your gear, you will need to start the bulk of the preparation. Research your guest and his or her field. The purpose of the interview sets your goals. To accomplish those objectives, you now will engage in research.

The most convenient source is the internet where using a search engine you can bring up multiple pages about your interview guest and his or her field. Remember, however, that information on the web is not necessarily trustworthy. Unlike traditional books that have been through a publisher's process of editing and fact checking, anyone can put anything on the web. Wikipedia is an example of this phenomena, and you will need to double check your online sources.

Don't forget about your local library for research. By going to the library, you will discover sources that are not necessarily on the web, and there is less chance that what you find is not factual in the books there. Remember you can use the librarians as a resource to help you in your searches. A trip to your local library may reward you with information you cannot find elsewhere.

Research your guest and his or her field and contributions. Be careful, however, because research is only research. You should use it to frame questions, not to write your story. What readers and viewers want is something beyond what they can find on their own, and my best interviews contained information that I did not find elsewhere.

The Subject Matter

When I prepared to interview Gordon Munro, I googled him on the web. What I learned was that he was heavily influenced by another famous fashion photographer, Irving Penn. I learned that early in his career he had served as an apprentice to Penn early in his career. I scoured the web to find out as much as I could about Penn and viewed a number of his photographs to get a feel for his style. I also looked at photos on the cover of fashion magazines like *Vogue*. This exploration helped me to understand my guest's environment.

I did a cursory look at the fashion industry, fashion photographers and those famous in other fields as well, lighting for portraits, and more. Although I did not directly use this information to build my list of questions, it helped me to feel more confident going into the interview since I was more informed about what he might say in his answers.

The Guest

My next step was to search for anything I could find about Gordon. I got an idea of his history and a deeper look into his style. From his own website, I learned he photographed both the famous and the not so famous. His pictures of Dustin Hoffman and Shirley MacLaine were warm and compelling. Portraits of unknown people were often taken with horses and dogs. All this information helped me to frame my questions. Although it was only during the interview that I learned how central horses were to his story, by knowing to ask about them, I was able to uncover the reason he moved from New York to the South.

With the availability of the web, information about your guest should be easy to obtain. As you do more research to conduct more interviews, you will become better at finding interesting material that will suggest questions. You have no excuse for not doing the research to be prepared. To do less is to be lazy, which likely means the interview will be average at best.

During my search I came across an article about conceptual art that was created and photographed by a Gordon Munro. This did not seem to fit into the profile I was gathering about him. One of my questions in the interview was about this unusual information, and I found that the person referred to was not the same Gordon Munro I was interviewing. This is another reason to use research as research. Until you verify what you have found, you cannot be sure that it is factual. Be sure your information is about your guest, and remember that anyone can put anything on the web. You are responsible for verifying whatever you present in your interview.

Notes

Drew Becker

Chapter 6
Why vs. Did You Know

Open and Closed Questions

When teaching a course about facilitation a number of years ago, I included the importance of knowing the difference between open and closed questions. I don't remember when I first learned about this. It was probably at some point in high school when I was not paying that much attention. Only later did this concept become important.

Closed Questions

As most of you know, closed questions can be answered with a simple "yes" or "no" or with a simple factual response. Questions like "Did you finish the work?" or "When did you finish the work?" do not require answers that uncover much other than a narrow response. The point of a closed question is to get a definite answer. This type of question is rarely useful when interviewing because it does not reveal the inner thoughts or feelings of the guest.

Closed questions are most useful in an investigative interview. In Mike Wallace's *60 Minutes* interviews where an interviewee (in this case not a guest) was confronted about an incident or about his or her company, closed questions focus on facts related to those inquiries.

Use a closed question to take control of the flow of an interview where the guest gets off track or rambles. Asking a question like "So you believe that the arts are flourishing in our city?" will redirect the guest and allow you to ask another question. You will want to be careful, however, not to shut down your guest with a closed question since the answer is usually a one-word response. Also, if he or she thinks you are not listening, don't want complete answers or have a bias you are trying to push, you can lose rapport that you spent time building up before and during the interview.

Open Questions

The answer to a well thought-out open question can reveal much about the guest and his or her opinions and character. This is because open questions are not directive; they do not ask the guest to answer in a certain way. The latitude of an open question allows someone to answer in an unstructured manner, and the way the guest reacts often is as telling as the answer itself. If I ask someone, "What was the inspiration behind this piece of art," the response could point to an influential person, could reach back into childhood, could reveal a forgotten conversation or any number of other things. The reply is interesting but the choice of how to answer may be even more compelling

Most open questions begin with why or how. To answer these questions, the guest shares the reasoning behind something or the process used to accomplish something else. These two questions can probe the most compelling revelations about your guest.

Why Is It...

Answers to why questions can help us understand psychological foundations about the guest, and as curious creatures our audience is fascinated by what drives a person. Haven't you often wondered why people do some of the things they do? One thing I always want to ask is why something has happened.

Asking why seems to be hardwired into our brains. Think about when you last spent time with a four-year old. At this age, we are natural investigators and the most prevalent question is why. If you look on the web, you will find that people believe four-year old children ask between 250-300 questions a day although those numbers may be an urban legend. No wonder parents are worn out by night time. Throughout our lives, we want to know reasons for many things.

How Do You Do?

The other significant question is how. This question asks the guest to share process. By inquiring how something came about or how the guest thought of an idea, we get a look inside, a quick flash into the reasoning, intuitive and/or creative process. These answers help our readers or viewers see into what makes the guest unique, fascinating and perhaps a master of his or her craft.

When I asked Gordon Munro, "How did you get into photography," he related the story of his career journey and his move to the United States from England, adding details and color along the way that enabled my readers to get to know him. The question also allowed him to share important life events that made him the photographer he is today.

In another interview, I asked a number of members of a work-out center, "How has coming to this facility helped you with your health" In each case the answers revealed the various benefits different people received. The question was easy to answer and indirectly spoke to one of the points we wanted to make in the testimonials.

Notes

Drew Becker

Chapter 7
What, When, Who? & Beyond

As stated previously, preparation is critical to a good interview. One of the elements of good preparation is compiling a list of questions. To do so, the interviewer has to research the guest and his or her area of expertise. I have found that I need to spend two to three times as much time doing research and preparing questions as I do conducting an interview. For a two-hour interview, I may spend five to six hours in preparation. Some of this time may be in the pre-interview session with a client and/or doing research on the web and in the library.

A significant amount of this time is dedicated to creating the basic list of questions to take into the interview with you. As a result it is beneficial to know about questions. In the last chapter, we began this investigation by discerning the difference between open and closed questions. Now, let's look at the categories of questions you can ask.

Many of you have heard about what is referred to as the five W's. These five classic questions that are taught in introduction to journalism classes along with an "H" question can cover most of the topics to be explored when interviewing. Some teachers now believe the five W's concept is passé, but these questions are still asked in many interviews even when they do not begin with one of the W's. Gaining knowledge through the five W's can fill in most of the meat of your interview.

The five W's (and H) are:

- Who
- What
- When
- Where
- Why
- How

Let's take a brief look at each to understand why these have been considered so important in the history of journalism and how mastering each of these types of questions can help you with your interviewing skills.

Who

The fundamental question is *Who*. We need to begin by letting the audience know who is being interviewed. *Who* questions can be answered in an introduction by the person running the interview or by the guest answering that query.

The Who question has more functions than simply identifying and getting to know the guest.

Other Who questions can help the interviewer and audience understand more about the subject of the interview.

- Who influenced you to become a _____(whatever the person is known for)?
- Who do others knowledgeable in your field consider experts?
- Who taught you the most important concepts?
- Who do you respect most in your field?
- Who would you be if you could be anyone else?

Who questions also can elicit information about other people related to your guest.

What

The next most important question is *What*. What questions cover a wide range of topics. They can set the parameter of the interview with an inquiry that refers to the topic of the interview, i.e., "What is it about photography that drew you to the field?" or even more generally, "What do you do?"

- What valuable information can you share about photography?
- What is the most important thing about lighting?
- What prompted you to do it (whatever created interest in you)?
- What makes you an authority in the field? (This also could be used for an introduction question.)
- What is your next project?

What questions cover a lot of territory; after all, they can set the scope for the entire interview or probe to a deep level. For example, a follow-up question like "What do you mean when you say..." creates a secondary, more in-depth inquiry. Another fantastic variation is the "What if..."

I find it interesting that all 10 of James Lipton's questions from the television show, *Inside the Actors Studio*, are what questions.[1]

When

When can be another important question while talking about future events. This has been part of the traditional 5W's and is useful in a press release because, along with who and what, this question elicits information critical for listeners or viewers who plan to attend an event.

There are, however, other times that this question can be useful:

- When is the art opening?
- When did you begin this project?
- When will your next project go public?
- When did you begin to see success?
- When did you first realize…?

Where

Where questions reveal location and also may refer to parts of a process or sequence.

- Where is your studio located?
- Where did the project start?
- Where is the performance?
- Where are the greatest risks and rewards? (This is a ephrasing of a what question.)

Why

Why inquiries are often the most revealing. Finding out the reasoning behind actions or understanding the feelings that prompted the guest to do something can help the reader or viewer get a deeper understanding of the person you interview.

- Why is this project important?
- Why do you prefer to do your work at night?
- Why did you start your business?
- Why do you use that process?

How

How questions help readers and viewers understand processes. When I ask how questions, my guests explain the manner in which they accomplish their work or the steps in the process.

- How do you set up a person for a great portrait?
- How many times did you have to experiment before it came out the way you wanted?
- How can a new photographer improve his or her pictures most easily?
- How can novices improve their pictures quickly?

How questions are great follow-ups to why questions. For example:

1. Why did you use platinum rather than silver in the finishing process of these photos?

2. How do you do that? How is it different from using silver?

By combining these two questions we learn not only about the motivation to use platinum but also something about how to do this kind of work. Both of these make for a rich understanding of the topic.

Miscellaneous

Other questions you might ask include:

- Do you ever consider...?
- If you could..., what would you do
- If you could..., how would you...?
- Have you ever...?
- Is there anything you would like to add?
- Describe...
- Share your thoughts about...
- Give me an example of...

Another important step is to order the questions so they build on one another. If the questions are well organized, the interview will flow more easily.

This discussion is the tip of the iceberg. Brainstorm your questions once you have done you research. As you do more interviews, building your questions and ordering them will become easier.

[1] https://creativepeeps.wordpress.com/2008/01/17/inside-the-actors-studio-10-questions/

Notes

Drew Becker

Chapter 8
Say What?

Once you begin the interview with a set of questions in your mind or written out, listen carefully to the answers. Responses can help you to determine the next question from your prepared list or to create important follow-up questions. What is exciting about an interview is that you, the interviewer, cannot predict all the answers. Good research will help you to have an idea what the guest will say, but when you get an answer you don't expect, you have a golden opportunity to take the interview in a different or deeper direction than you originally planned.

The Art of Listening

In everyday life, most people are so busy thinking what they will say next, that they lose track of what the other person is saying. As new interviewers conduct their sessions, they have a tendency to think ahead too much. When you are busy considering your next question, chances are you will miss some of what your guest is saying.

All great interviewers are excellent listeners. They are familiar enough with their questions (thanks to thorough preparation) that they can concentrate fully on their guest's responses. These people develop the skill of being fully attentive and preparing the next question as they listen.

Being fully attentive means not only listening to the words but also lbeing aware of the tone. Tone is the way we say what we are saying—modulations in voice and pace. Beyond tone, accomplished interviewers are watching for visual signals that reveal what the guest is really saying or may be hiding. These visual cues are comprised of body language and facial expressions. Body language includes how the guests sit and the way they hold their necks, legs, arms and hands. Facial expressions expose the emotions behind the words.

In Julian Fast's classic, *Body Language*, written in 1970, he talks about how many aspects of the unconscious and one's culture are revealed in the way we hold our bodies. He describes how our personal appearance and choice of clothing send messages about us as well. He talks about genuine and not-so-genuine smiles and about postures, revealing what it means when someone crosses arms and/or legs. All these signals, many unconscious, are messages. If you are not familiar with works about body language, you might look into it because recognizing these gestures and expressions can make you a better interviewer.

The television series *Lie to Me,* which ran from 2009-2011, was about a group of consultants who conducted difficult investigations and arrived at the truth by observing and reacting to what are called micro expressions. The methods used on the show were an adaptation of the work of Paul Ekman and Wallace Friesen, who wrote several books including *Unmasking the Face.* The book describes these micro expressions for six emotions: anger, disgust, fear, happiness, sadness and surprise. By observing the interviewee's micro expressions—short facial expressions less than 1/5 of a second—the consultants could determine whether they were lying or telling the truth. Watching the series enabled the viewer to become more conscious of these brief expressions.

A good interviewer will be looking for these as well as body language because part of attentive listening is visual. Even if you are not skilled at reading micro expressions, observing as you are listening and paying attention to the guest rather than yourself will make you a better interviewer.

Another communication strategy you might want to get familiar with, if you are not already, is reflective listening. This consists of hearing the answer and then reporting back. You do not have the use the stilted, "I heard you say..." but could reflect. "Then you think..., right?"

Don't Get Locked in

Although I recommend that you prepare adequate questions, don't let those questions imprison you. It is tempting to want to ask everything on your list since you spent all that time doing research, but that may not be feasible or wise for a number of reasons.

I usually leave an interview without using all of my questions. This may happen because of time limitations or because the interview has taken a different direction and the questions are not as important or relevant as I thought they would be. I rarely regret omitting the questions. If the interview is for print and you need to follow up with one or more of those questions, you can always send an email request.

Listen for Follow-up

What do you do when an answer suggests there is an interesting area for which you have not prepared a question? You ask a new one, of course. Since you will have to think on your feet to compose the question, be sure it is not a closed question if you want more than a brief answer.

If you want to know more about a process, ask a how-type question. To learn more about the emotions or thoughts behind something said, use a why or how question.

- Why do you think that?
- How did that make you feel?
- How did you react?

To clarify an answer, you might ask for a definition of a term or statement.

- What did you mean when you said…?
- What does (the term) mean to you?
- How are you using the term (word)?
- Did I understand you when you said...?
- Was that in Illinois or in North Carolina?

You also may want to reflect back to the guest to be sure you understood.

- I heard you say... Is that what you meant/said?
- Let me be sure I got the point...
- Did you say…?

At times you may have to regain control when your guest does not answer the question but starts talking about something else.

- Repeat the question.
- I'm not sure I understand, (Repeat the question.)
- I see. What were you saying about (the original topic)?
- If he or she gives you a generic answer, ask "How does

that affect you?"

Sometimes I will let the guest talk a bit about whatever topic he or she uses to dodge my question because he or she may inadvertently answer or give me another opening to approach that topic. Be sure you get the whole story with good follow-up questions.

Notes

Drew Becker

Chapter 9
The Answers

OK, so now you know your purpose and goals, you've set up a time and place for your meeting, decided what kind of interview to do, done your research, prepared your list of questions, gathered your equipment, and arrived for the interview or set it up digitally. Now you are ready to begin.

Last Minute Tips

Here are a few hints that will take your interview from ordinary to spectacular.

Make it unique. Earlier I stated that you do not want to rehash what is already out on the web. Find your special slant and way to conduct an interview that is distinctly you. As an interviewer you want to create that personal brand that is recognizable in all your interviews. This does not necessarily mean wearing a red hat or sitting in a certain way, but more often, is a reflection of the person you are that will bring out something in your guest that others might not be able to elicit.

The discussion should be only about the guest, not about the interviewer. Don't overpower your guest; let him or her be the star. If you are too busy showing how great you are, your listening skills will be hampered, and your guests may not want to compete with your strong personality to impart their information. Remind yourself of your purpose.

Make sure you are genuine when you do the interview. Approach from an honest point of view and avoid a strong bias. Otherwise your audience will be limited to those who share the same perspective. Be fair in the way you ask questions and allow your guest to complete answers. Combative interviews don't usually work—especially in person—as well as they appear to on television.

Your interviewees are your guests. Treat them with respect whether you agree with what they say or not. Your audience is smart; if you are right and your guest is wrong, they can figure it out. Do not interrupt except when absolutely necessary—when a guest is way off track or yammers on and on. In those cases, kindly lead them back with the right question.

Only answer when it is necessary. Your audience will tire of your conversational responses such as, "right" or "I see" in an audio or video interview. Be silent and let the guest speak. By not responding to each comment, you also will have more time to listen and to prepare your next question.

At the Interview

You are now seated across from your guest or looking at one another on webcams. Once you have gotten the technical considerations out of the way, take a deep breath yourself and help your guest get comfortable. Have a few minutes of casual conversation. Depending on the guest and the time allotted for the interview, this could take from one minute to 20 minutes. When I was interviewed on a radio show, the host asked me to come in 30 minutes early. We settled in and talked for about 15 minutes before the program. This put me at ease.

Remember to smile. Interviewers can become so intent on getting a good interview that they forget to smile. This is a good icebreaker and, while smiling, communications are easier to listen to and watch.

Right before the interview or video shoot, you can help your guest by discussing wardrobe and makeup,where he or she will be seated, standing or staged and where to look and speak. Reiterate how long it will take to set up, the four to five questions you will ask (bring an extra copy), how you will conduct the interview and what you will do to end it.

Set up your guest somewhere he or she is comfortable. If filming, you may have to move things around to get a good background and depth for the shot. By placing a prop in the shot at a different distance from the interviewee, you will create a more realistic looking video. Once the scene is set, talk casually before beginning. Let the person know that you want him or her talking to you, not performing for the camera. Be sure you both have water nearby and are not thirsty or have dry mouth before beginning. Just before starting I like to ask my guest to stand or sit with good posture, get comfortable and inhale and exhale a few times.

Begin with an introduction of your guest or ask the guest either by you or the inteviewee. I prefer to introduce the person because it lets the guest have another minute or two to get settled. In your preparations, you should have asked for a written bio or information to create one that you can use to begin the interview.

Be sure to define any terms you use during the interview. I often will ask a question to get the guest's definition of a word or acronym. Be sure your audience knows what acronyms and industry-specific terms mean. This will give them an understanding as your guest talks about that topic.

Ask your questions clearly and concisely, and keep them simple. The answers can be complex but great questions are usually straightforward. Focus on the guest. Don't show what a great interviewer you are by taking up time and explaining to the guest how much you know about him or her. Remember to keep the emphasis on the person you are interviewing.

Many first-time interviewers want to show how much they know. This ego-driven behavior or the nervousness that creates it can unsettle your guest. You are not there to impress anyone but to draw out information, emotion and personality. You want the viewer or reader to experience the person you are interviewing. Your personality will come through naturally if you are being yourself. Viewers or readers will understand who you are by the questions you ask and the way the guest interacts with you.

Listen carefully to responses. One answer often can lead to another question that delves deeper into the topic and enriches the session. When your guest feels he or she is truly being heard, he or she often shares more. One of the lost treasures of modern life is being listened to and really heard. When I interview people, some love to tell me things they have held back previously. When they realize I am really listening, the gems roll out.

After the connection is made, you can ask some of the more challenging questions, and I have found I can then get those answers with little resistance. If I ask too early, though, I get no answer or only brief, curt responses.

Finally, be sure to thank the guest after the interview. Even if you are being paid to do the session, the person has given you time. Being grateful may open the door for future opportunities with this person or referrals for more interviews with others..

Afterward

If you are writing your interview, complete a first draft as soon as possible. The fresher the conversation is in your mind, the easier it will be to write. If you have created a video or sound interview that will be edited, do so as quickly as possible as well. The longer you wait, the easier it is to procrastinate finishing the project. If your interview was live, you have no post production activities.

When I have time, I like to send a note or email thanking my guest. It is a courtesy and makes him or her feel special.

Take a breath and enjoy the experience you have just had. Ask yourself some questions to review the process:

- What went well?
- What part of the interview was most fun?
- What part could I have done better?
- How can I improve?

By answering these questions, you can improve your game for the next interview. You also will become more at ease the next time and in turn make your guests more comfortable.

Notes

Drew Becker

Chapter 10
Can we Get a Checklist?

I have divided the check list into four parts: Preparation, Pre-Interview, Interview and Post Interview.

Checklist

Preparation tasks

- ☐ Determine the purpose.
- ☐ What goals will lead to fulfilling that purpose?
- ☐ Who is your audience?
- ☐ Are there any language restrictions? If so what are they?
- ☐ Conduct the pre-interview session.
- ☐ Research your guest and topic.
- ☐ Write your questions.

Pre-Interview tasks

- [ ] Give your guest a list of some of the questions and explain there may be more.

- [ ] Discuss logistics:

    - ◊ Length of interview

    - ◊ Time and date

    - ◊ Number of people who will be there

    - ◊ Equipment

- [ ] Determine acceptable and non-acceptable topics.

- [ ] Ask for a bio or take notes to write an introduction.

- [ ] Get all necessary releases signed.

- [ ] Discuss what setup will be done on the day of the interview if any.

- [ ] Talk about what to wear for a video interview.

At the Interview tasks

- ☐ Arrive at least 15-30 minutes ahead.
- ☐ Bring the introduction.
- ☐ Bring makeup for live video.
- ☐ Bring Equipment. * See listings below.

Post Interview

- ☐ Send a thank you note or email.
- ☐ Keep track of your written interview due date: _____.
- ☐ Stick to your sound interview editing completion date _____.
- ☐ Set and honor your video editing completion date: _____.

Equipment Lists

Written Interview

- Pencils/Pens
- Paper/legal pad
- Padfolio
- Computer or laptop
- Digital Voice Recorder

Audio Interview

- Digital Voice Recorder
- Microphone if not internal for recorder
- Pencils/Pens
- Paper/legal pad
- Padfolio
- Computer or laptop
- Electrical cords
- Extension cords
- Pick up for telephone (for phone interviews)

Video Interview- Web

- Computer or laptop
- Webcam and software- the higher the quality the better
- Microphone
- Reliable fast internet connection—preferably hard wired
- Video calling software
    - ◊ Google account with Hangouts
    - ◊ Skype
    - ◊ Others
- Pencils/Pens
- Paper/legal pad
- Padfolio

Video Interview Live

- Video camera
- Microphones
- Tripod
- Connecting cables
- Extension cords
- Gaffers tape
- Lights and light stands

- On board lights
- Pencils/Pens
- Paper/legal pad
- Padfolio
- Computer or laptop

Chapter 11
Last Words

Thank you for purchasing this book. I appreciate your support. Now you have the basics to conduct a great interview. Practice makes perfect; if you haven't begun, get started now. If you have, go do another interview and see how these tips might help. Please also go to the link in the back of this book to get updates and special offers. When you come on board, I will email you a bonus.

I am always interested in what my readers think, feel free to email me at info@drewbecker.com.

To get the most recent updates to the book and to comment, go to *http://drewbecker.com/?p=996*

Other books by Drew Becker

I Fell for 13 Dreamers

Write a Non-Fiction Book in 4 Weeks

www.ingramcontent.com/pod-product-compliance
Lightning Source LLC
Chambersburg PA
CBHW071725020426
42333CB00017B/2396